FESTIVAL OF DOOM

Playwright

by

Baruch Menache

New York, NY

United States of America

© 2025 Baruch Menache

Published by McWest & Associates

All rights reserved. ISBN: 978-1-971928-44-9

SETTING AND TIME

The play unfolds across beaches, roads, inns, towns, camps, and festivals.

The time is indeterminate; suggestive of a pre-modern or mythic landscape, unbound to a fixed historical period.

DRAMATIS PERSONAE

Davenport
A traveler of reflection and inward contest.

Cody
A companion of wit, charm, and veiled resolve.

Donnatella
A woman of presence, instinct, and changing allegiance.

Timothy
An observer, agitator, and bearer of unsettling
commentary.

The Governor
A figure of authority and seduction.

The Bartender

The Waiter

The Chorus
A collective voice of passage, memory, and aftermath.

ACT 1: FRIENDSHIP IS MADE

[On the beach, chanced encounter, walking next to their horses]

DAVENPORT:

>Don't I know you?
>
>You seem familiar enough.

CODY:

>A lover?
>
>Maybe, capable of love—surely.
>
>Sensible enough, cared for the young; maybe,
>
>Your face is plentitude of youthful glare.

DAVENPORT:

>Late dreams that void interpretation
>
>Abashed this sentimentality of faith.
>
>Charisma cherished whence staled,
>
>Noticed and adored; to what gateway?
>
>Early morning is better kept in darkness.

CODY:

>Frequenting the same repose
>
>Entering by way of stables;
>
>Front door that steals charm,

Gratuity as a trait to mention.

DAVENPORT:

Scorned use-traits for the beholder

That cannot measure if never sold.

Chosen boldly, frowned upon disfavor

Of never staking ground to a spoken word.

CODY:

Smile told at birth, jittery is mine own way.

Delight minus creamer sufficed your grace.

Shall we lead your path of inquiry!

Scatter away the remaining years?

Arguing in favor of disfavor?

Inconclusive been given a name;

The true coward of us all.

DAVENPORT:

Ha! Spoken without response,

Sent back to be spoken again.

If I twofold, three would be no harm.

Skilled without a performer,

A trait without a tradesman.

Faithless journey for a path harkened end,

Sipping wine at this festival of doom, shan't you be next?

The abysmal state of an in-between.

A crack in your smile

Shan't censor the illusion.

Born to a frown, a smile to a pose

Without the ever-daring response;

It is I who remains the coward.

Rest in this namesake,

'till other folk can spake thy name.

CODY:

You find favor in response

With no charm to a final fix.

Here goes the tale,

Journey'd maiden,

Vetoed alongside.

Do enjoy its sand,

Dreary they come along

Singing a song of unity,

Careless to the end;

Its solitude gives you right.

If ever there was a response

You'd never hear twice.

To another mate found

With fewer smiles than me.

[Davenport Turning]

Ah! Already on your way?

DAVENPORT:

No, sir, to hear you loud is all

In noise that befalls a word or two

That solitude ought never multiply.

I make amends to folk in-kind

Bearing whatever the way,

Chanced if I'd walk alone.

When in all my grace

It is made known in truth.

Alone is to go when favor aghast,

Redeem me now, be my better way!

CODY:

Taking a liking!

First charm is much,

A smile; a sure incentive.

Favor that redeems your spell!

DAVENPORT:

You have made known the concealed,

In this I'll admit: enjoy youth's share.

Let us travel together as my retreat.

[They leave together on horseback and begin the journey]

Act 2: The Girl

WAITER:

> Try the tiramisu that softens its lot,
>
> Hunger to road, filled in layover,
>
> Respite is travel to the wheels.
>
> Take a try, a bite—a must.

DAVENPORT:

> We'd try another night
>
> In this meal unearned.
>
> Fable the dish sure to its maker,
>
> Smells the quarter, entreats the king.

CODY:

> Why haven't the delight—if offered?
>
> Trust—it might get you thru the night.

DAVENPORT:

> A laugh is shy from a tear,
>
> Dime costed the nickel;
>
> Lone choice for any objective,
>
> Mine-aim is center-sight.

Periphery and the distracted margin;

Red-block complexion, paged surreal.

WAITER:

When matches ignite the matchbox,

Supposed the destroyer of its remedy.

Colden' dish merits the heat,

Passion roasted the chicken,

Dried for amicable dessert.

[Put up his hands]

I'll leave the remark in fold,

Over there I'll wait the charge.

[Waiter leaves]

[Overhearing them at the other table, another patron]

DONNATELLA:

Paraded your abstinence,

Church goers carry note,

Fathers' retold of scolded earth.

Hail you from, thought not from here?

WAITER:

[Interrupting, referencing the girl]

Weather dripping rain in portico,

Plants watered, maiden showered.

Grass thicker in the near,

Save for a grazed vista.

Donnatella is called by the mistress,

How she adores that name in myth.

DONNATELLA:

> Bonds are molded in ice and dirt,
>
> Tangled of childhood webs.
>
> Stable towns and ghosted memories,
>
> Some for a smile to honor the tear;
>
> Others to seek misery and its chance.
>
> To whom makes this bond unique?

CODY:

> Each is a journey'd unfold,
>
> Friendship founded en-route
>
> If ever friendship is not found this way.

DAVENPORT:

> A matter of convenience is one-and-two;
>
> Coupled in hardship and in love.
>
> Besides the saddle that counts in twos,
>
> Wheels of four for backs of two.

DONNATELLA:

> Sounds the better of men,
>
> Changes clothes with times.
>
> Better be offered a repeat,
>
> To the tavern is their lot.
>
> Complaining the state of world,
>
> As younglings read not yet speak of coal,

Girls taken a liking to a waged worker;

And your objective, as it may be told?

CODY:

The lacquered item that glows with perchance,

Been told of the gem of man,

Searching the high-low for the low-high.

A relic or two of nature, crusted history's stamp.

An art dealer in looks of works, or a lover of man

In looks of character and wise adages.

DAVENPORT:

Oh, a very wise articulation,

Shan't the sales of the estate

Be a bounty twofold for that orator.

Given a girl chance to profess interest,

'stead of offering bread before water.

DONNATELLA:

The likeness of you two

Standing on the same rock.

Where this journey unfold?—

Business is made in Pocochella.

DAVENPORT:

Afar from Canterbury Wood,

That be two clicks apart,

Shan't you accompany to camp?

DONNATELLA:

I am obliged.

[They go to sleep, she travels with them the next day]

ACT 3: ENTER POCOCHELLA

[On their way, as they enter Pocochella]

DAVENPORT:

> There is value to price
>
> In wind-habits abroad,
>
> Miles stretched of innocence,
>
> Exiled in all its glamour—

[Noticing the abundant farmland]

DONNATELLA:

> Exclude the foreigner pledged to sight.
>
> Homage costs the price of love,
>
> Or haven't you seen love in a public square?—
>
> It's a wonder any child is born at all.

DAVENPORT:

> Child is a rescue of parental misstep,
>
> Some call miracle; others, nature's part.
>
> Cherish what the eye sees
>
> Over what the heart knows;
>
> Never has the child cried a gift unwrapping.

[Passing even more abundant farmland]

CODY:

> Steel-footed ground, crops in plenty;
>
> None to eat, only to sustain.
>
> Safe haven in the quarterly,
>
> Denied a second dispatch.

[They hear the chatter of the town]

> Trusting instinctual sounds
>
> Made in cold buffers,
>
> Forestalling their way to Mother.

DONNATELLA:

> Sampled a taste of evergreen oak,
>
> Tables do work that can't be undone.
>
> Scratchy silence is the right approach—
>
> Fleece and linen taken for a wash.

TIMOTHY:

> Fickle at the sidewalk,
>
> Training eyes bespoke harmony.
>
> They'd know by now —
>
> That evergreen is spelled with e's
>
> And trees creep up on summer.

GATEKEEPER:

> Went Father to his flock
>
> That made known their silence.
>
> It was distrust indeed—
>
> As man had known before,
>
> Or rather, learned in pain;
>
> White rose lead the way!

[They enter the city]

[Gatekeepers friend Timothy follow them in]

> Tricked by solace,
>
> Ivory bridge—bottlenecked;
>
> Breathless entanglements of merit.

[He screams out to them]

> Going to run for mayor
>
> To delight my species of cattle;
>
> Sheep and goats; milk from udders.

[Gatekeeper turns back]

TIMOTHY:

> And those unearthed
>
> For the florist's game
>
> Have prickly cut out — never.

[Seeing the aghast at his pessimism]

> Never a reminder of its faith
>
> And how it passes for love!

DAVENPORT:

> A rebellion of nature
>
> Said in deference of words,
>
> Threaded in sentences,
>
> Weighed in memory.
>
> To be filled again
>
> With more prose than captures.

Shuttered Francesca

To an oversized windbreaker.

DONNATELLA:

Safe—

In the reminder of pain

As if some kind of holder.

CODY:

Deli-wax and picky-wags

Set buzzing on said tree

Eating foliage at rates

Bygone to its counterpart.

[They all enter the town tavern]

ACT 4: TAVERN

BARTENDER:

> Sidebarred to a closet, olden clothes possessed.
>
> Faraway to scour the checked club—
>
> Where goes the chancellor bearing the name?
>
> Covers more ground than walking, short of distance.

DAVENPORT:

> Mustn't we pull the mask to encounter the subject?
>
> Subject angled in some way fit,
>
> Carved for a microscopic lens.
>
> Eyed to taste, envied and accessed—
>
> No need for chivalry.
>
> Folk had honor as badged confidence,
>
> Living to reply a rejoinder,
>
> Solved the mystery of loss
>
> Without a lively search 'n rescue.

BARTENDER:

Return Civilization to her owners.

Take their wine and cheese—

To talk! To speak—what for?

DONNATELLA:

When ravaging food-supply is defeat,

Humbling in the direction of famine.

Eating less than a mammalian share,

Stoking love in debt to a westward dove.

The fruitful reply is their mode of necessity.

Take my abundance, sir,

I have more coming my way.

Take the lot, for there is an allowance.

They'd come in many ways, cumbersome in all,

They'd open their horizon to the very few

To show prowess and engender the state.

BARTENDER:

With color they make sounds,

With acrylics they make paint.

Never has art seen such genius;

Never have the theologians

When cryptic messaging come to play.

TIMOTHY:

Sampled goods exposed,

Secondary market—the streets.

CODY:

Free to the one who begs,

Weighty to the cherished eye.

The stupor, shrouded from throbbing,

Colorless heaven adjourned the occasion.

Did you find justification after all?

By the overgrown bush

Across the bike lane

Where trespassers go;

The emblem of residence.

Come by the West side;

The sun—east expenses the shadow

Which scares the child all the same;

Triumph the blade of grass.

DONNATELLA:

> The sound-wind blows,
>
> Fateful to the howling faceless,
>
> Never made known their name nor mark,
>
> Feared the suspicion when man 's to blame.

ACT 5: NEXT TOWN

DAVENPORT:

> Didactic prodigy in a learning train,
>
> Given word to form a posture,
>
> Knows way from maps,
>
> Of roads, people, and things.
>
> Color-coded, straight 'n edgy lines,
>
> Written to scale and proportion.

TIMOTHY:

> It is rather a right or left;
>
> Two directions for all things,
>
> Styled a gathering in form,
>
> Baseless at the fruit budding.

CODY:

> Mirror-glass upholds the hunchback,
>
> Telling a feeling proves ill a sensation,
>
> Proved the world in a single handshake.

DONNATELLA:

> Merits leverage to the fragility of old,

Situated where oceans are scarce

And ladies do just as they're told.

Dare show me that yellow hat,

Brushed skin to the detriment of all,

Keep aback, four paces for yellow.

DAVENPORT:

Trust the overachievers with a tale of stars;

The unders, for a tale of scars;

All else, save for a tale.

ACT 6: JOURNEY

[In the long journey from Pocochella, they grow tired, camping the night in the wilderness, around the fire]

TIMOTHY:

> Terrace-green veiled home,
>
> Fenced to a neighboring scream.
>
> Told of fancy, missed its mark.
>
> Scolded by a kitchen flame,
>
> Choice'd food served in style,
>
> French arranged, States disguised.

CODY:

> Sensed a data reserve
>
> Bespoke of memory.
>
> Directed in love of identity,
>
> Tipped a hat in deference.

DONNATELLA:

> Fractions in rations, amiss a girl amongst,
>
> Brethren grasped in blackened war.
>
> A maiden fright, then again, her smile,
>
> Carved a girl in enemy camp; she's never the same.
>
> Await a sensation that knows beyond this game.

[She leaves camp, cleans herself, adorn to the best and then returns]

Fright, it is true, for now you see,

To serve fear of tested men,

Showing nimble your title.

Come now, tea and stories,

The feat of boot takes rest.

[Change of mood, they drink and merry, stories]

TIMOTHY:

Fiction, I'll tell you, Derosa of Madahorn was sure gone by

In a righteous son to lead and lady to detest exile,

Deserved the fate of his blow, finds bosom in the enemy.

CODY:

Said truer words never,

Madahorn must be proud,

Shame of King betrayed,

Departed the single man forest,

To tell a city its unsanctioned descent.

A dreary love on the other side,

Derosa, dare I say, Barbarossa and be gone!

[Davenport takes a view to Donnatella, sits together on the sidelines]

DAVENPORT:

[Quietly]

> Fare you with mischievous trite,
>
> Accompany a stranger, consent a friend.
>
> Gestured awaiting the tree,
>
> As lady 'tella' adorns 'donna.'

DONNATELLA:

> Of all men in defenses
>
> Choice is deferred to nethermost crop,
>
> In wheat than barley, goat to cow's utters.
>
> Nature smirks to a determinate gesture,
>
> Irony played in its own field of toys.
>
> Each will have their fear,
>
> None of war can set it free.
>
> Lady—I am, standing erect,
>
> Mongering more than a-thousand archery,
>
> Tenfold of cavalry—iron-made.

DAVENPORT:

> Daring a timepiece
>
> Clocking rhythmic beats.
>
> Sadness softens bagged eyes;

He's the soldier playing pawns,

In king's cheap pastime,

Proud, aloof, lost to pain;

Artist to describe humankind.

Fastened to sea, traversing thoughts,

Hope for another time

And another expanse.

Where sailors are younger,

And pilot is new with ideas;

Passengers delight their reflection.

Sorrow keeps this ocean liner afloat;

And the day of too much happiness

Brings a bearing of weather.

Know that it is not ocean or land,

But the exchange of passenger and sailor,

Sailor to pilot

And pilot to God.

[Timothy leaves]

ACT 7: THE FESTIVAL

[In the height of spirit, at the festival, a governor approaches the group]

GOVERNOR:

> Say, misses of the great festival,
>
> Shine this way, favor is on hold.
>
> Thrice gave plenty, awaiting a ready score.
>
> Winner to the games placed at its lead

DONNATELLA:

> Fare you sir, I've been told,
>
> Mystery is found in chance,
>
> Never to question its coming.

GOVERNOR:

> Dealed a similar fate
>
> In quest of direction,
>
> A face was shown
>
> More beautiful than you.

DONNATELLA:

> I fear the heart of a lady is weak,
>
> In the hearing of a goodness streak,
>
> Turning back to the avail.

GOVERNOR:

> Contrarian to what's told,
>
> Beauty was known two-minutes to date,
>
> In the cumber tent, in the pane stood a dame,
>
> Only later it was known in grand name,
>
> 'Tella to Donna, it is sure but you, Donnatella.

DONNATELLA:

> Spirited this clever ransom
>
> Makes worth of lengthy days,
>
> Grants amnesty of a grieving heart.
>
> Utopia seems nearer now,
>
> Future blast in kind words exchanged
>
> Scrambling dearest plans,
>
> Poaches busy, cuts her in half.

GOVERNOR:

> She is now a taken bride,
>
> A wish that is never stale.

[She leaves the group, locks arms with the governor and doesn't say farewell]

ACT 8: THE FESTIVAL-ENDING

[At the festival]

DAVENPORT:

> Picked that jacket, told you of the other,
>
> Getting right for nimble minds,
>
> Sanity is no rest in corruptin' favor,
>
> Fox'd me a lion stare;
>
> Gazelle in hairlock.

CODY:

> Spoken this angry chew
>
> Gone is that smile,
>
> Taken its rightful abode,
>
> Done the truth already,
>
> To care in spite of hurt.

DAVENPORT:

> Fine by me.
>
> Truss and twist—
>
> Gavel'd a friendship.
>
> Words, tongued in spears,
>
> Defenseless to pursuit.
>
> The enemy is the known face;

The wary friend is masked.

Pick'd a side that hasn't the role

Wherewithal to the uninvited.

CODY:

[Softly]

I'll find you in the dead winter,

Whence cold catches puny toes.

Brazen is a forgotten memory,

In shiny sun we absolve disfavor.

You see more than me—and I, you.

Were never more than a chariot wheel

Chasing the sea-faring ghost.

Love is found in temper,

In a blast—we are to depart.

Shan't it be anything of love

To be called a memory?

DAVENPORT:

Fox—you, fox!

Hadn't the decency to show face

As temper thinned and girl gone,

In two-week journey at sea,

Giving thought a chance of rest.

You forget your nature

And sow pockets on dresses.

CODY:

Catch a drift at sea,

I'll know better the rotten course

That'll give time

To a precious love of heart.

In all colors,

I'll see you black.

Deep in winter shelter,

I'll see the melting snow

Dripping from foliage.

DAVENPORT:

Crack a window

To get a breather.

Be the bird who knows feathers;

The mountain goat in good pasture.

Carve the rebellion in better enemies,

Find disgust in your veneer.

Personage of discord to territorial claim.

Did I ask for a dime?

Or a nickel of respite?

Adorned your shine;

Better than the prowling sun.

In nighttime, full moon served less.

CODY:

[Near whisper]

Guessin' love shields a commonplace,

Fixed the sample of goodness

Alone with solitude, a man's passion.

DAVENPORT:

For resurrection 'tis a willful blow

More earthly than a free favor.

Epilogue:

Chorus:

Captain brimmed with wine,

Sailors aback the engine room

Waves crash the hulk,

Deck covered in fresh rainwater.

Two ladies, gin and tonic;

Memory is all they have.

Three letters sit to be opened,

Daring passengers, forgotten land,

An approximate smile is all to be had.

Shelter in the iron rock,

Swaying to and fro.

[Soaked package of letters, letter two writes:]

Daring fellow that makes rain a jest,

A storm from the east warms my heart,

Drifting salt and the smell of oceans,

Friendship is the watery pain of a stormy ocean day.

To a life of plenty, dessert is its first course,

Rancid is the ending that knows not love,

If favor is your last utter, than mine is ado.

About the Author

Baruch Menache writes at the intersection of narrative, philosophy, and lyric expression. His work spans poetry, essays, and theatrical pieces that examine the interior life and its many thresholds. He lives in New York with his Wife and Children.